Empower

Publishing

WATCH FOR MORE TITLES
FROM PATRICIA HARRISON

AND *EMPOWER PUBLISHING*

SO MUCH LOVE INSIDE:

POETRY FROM THE SOUL OF A WOMAN

BY

PATRICIA M. HARRISON

EMPOWER PUBLISHING
WINSTON-SALEM

EMPOWER PUBLISHING
302 RICKS DRIVE
WINSTON-SALEM, NC 27103

THE OPINIONS EXPRESSED IN THIS WORK ARE ENTIRELY THE OPINIONS OF THE AUTHOR AND DO NOT REPRESENT THE OPINIONS OR THOUGHTS OF THE PUBLISHER. THE AUTHOR HAS REPRESENTED AND WARRANTED ALL OWNERSHIP AND/OR LEGAL RIGHT TO PUBLISH ALL THE MATERIALS IN THIS BOOK.

COPYRIGHT 2023 BY PATRICIA M. HARRISON

ALL RIGHTS RESERVED, INCLUDING THE RIGHT OF REPRODUCTION IN WHOLE OR PART IN ANY FORMAT.

FIRST EMPOWER PUBLISHING BOOKS EDITION PUBLISHED
MARCH, 2024
EMPOWER PUBLISHING, FEATHER PEN, AND ALL PRODUCTION DESIGN ARE TRADEMARKS.

FOR INFORMATION REGARDING BULK PURCHASES OF THIS BOOK, DIGITAL PURCHASE AND SPECIAL DISCOUNTS, PLEASE CONTACT THE PUBLISHER AT PUBLISH.EMPOWER.NOW@GMAIL.COM

COVER DESIGN BY PAN MORELLI
MANUFACTURED IN THE UNITED STATES OF AMERICA
ISBN 978-1-63066-583-8

ABOUT THE AUTHOR

PATRICIA HARRISON IS A PUBLISHED POET WHO HAS WON MANY AWARDS FOR HER POETRY INCLUDING SILVER POET AWARDS, GOLDEN POET AWARDS, AWARD OF MERIT CERTIFICATE AND A WHO'S WHO IN POETRY HONOR. SHE BEGAN WRITING THIS ANTHOLOGY OF POETRY IN 1989 AND FOUND HERSELF CONTINUING TO WRITE UNTIL THIS BOOK WAS PUBLISHED.

FOR MORE THAN HALF HER LIFE, PATRICIA HAS DEDICATED HER TIME TO WRITING POETRY, SUSPENSE, AS WELL AS CHILDREN'S STORIES AS A HOBBY. AT THE URGING OF THOSE CLOSE TO HER, SHE HAS DECIDED TO SHARE HER LITERARY WORKS WITH OTHERS.

PATRICIA BELIEVES LOVE, TRUTH AND PEACE ARE ESSENTIAL TO HAPPINESS AND HOPES THAT HER WRITINGS WILL INSPIRE THE SAME IN HER READERS.

A SPECIAL THANKS

TO MY FAMILY AND FRIENDS FOR ALL THE LOVE AND SUPPORT SHOWN THROUGHOUT THE CREATION OF THIS BOOK.

ALSO, A SPECIAL THANKS TO SANTENNA WOO. THANKS, SANTENNA, FOR YOUR EXTRODINARY EFFORTS AS WELL AS THE BEAUTIFUL COVER DESIGN CONCEPT.

ABOVE ALL

I GIVE THANKS TO GOD/ALLAH FOR BLESSING ME WITH THE GIFT THAT ALLOWS ME TO INSPIRE.

LOVE AND PEACE TO ALL FOREVER

—PATRICIA

TO MY READERS:

"SO MUCH LOVE INSIDE" IS A COLLECTION OF POETRY WHICH EXPRESSES MY INNER THOUGHTS, BARES MY SOUL AND TELLS OF THE DEPTH OF MY LOVE. IT TELLS NOT ONLY OF LOVE IN CONJUNCTION WITH BEING IN LOVE, IT ALSO TELLS OF MY ABILITY TO LOVE AND BE LOVED.

MY LOVE RUNS DEEP. MY LOVE POURS FROM THE DEPTHS OF MY HEART AND FLOWS THROUGH THE VERY STREAMS OF MY VEINS. IT KEEPS MY BODY ALIVE. THAT'S HOW DEEP MY LOVE IS. I LOVE YOU, MY READERS, MY FAMILY, NATURE AND ITS WONDERS AND, OF COURSE, I LOVE THE CHILDREN. I LOVE THE CHILDREN WITH EVERY BREATH I TAKE BECAUSE THEY ARE MY TOMORROW. LAST, BUT NOT LEAST, I LOVE MYSELF. LOVE OF ONESELF IS A LIFETIME NECESSITY AND WILL PROPEL US THROUGH THE HARDEST OF TIMES.

IT IS MY DESIRE THAT MY POETRY WILL INSPIRE NOTHING BUT LOVE IN THE HEARTS OF MY READERS. BE IT LOVE OF ANIMALS, OR LOVE FOR MAN OR WOMAN, LET THERE BE LOVE. WHERE THERE IS LOVE, THERE IS PEACE, AND WHERE THERE IS PEACE THERE IS HAPPINESS. LET LOVE PREVAIL.

—PATRICIA M. HARRISON

TABLE OF CONTENTS

THOUGHT FOR THE DAY	1
TEACH OUR BABIES	3
SEND ME A BOUQUET	5
PRETENDING	7
ABUSED CHILD	9
THOUGHT FOR THE DAY	11
LITTLE ONE	13
MY AMAZING SPECIAL NEEDS CHILD	15
A CHILD	17
THOUGHT FOR THE DAY	19
WHAT IS A WOMAN	21
RESPECT	23
AFTER THE BREAKUP	25
SISTERS	27
DOMESTIC ABUSE	29
JUST LEAVE	31
IT'S JUST ME (AND I LOVE IT!)	33
JUST THAT KIND OF GIRL	35
THOUGHT FOR THE DAY	37
FOREVER YOU	39
LOVE IS ON THE WAY	41
THE DARKER THE FLESH, THE DEEPER I LOVE	43
PEANUT BUTTER MAN	45
THE THIEF	47
WHERE ARE THE GOOD BLACK MEN	49
JOB WELL DONE	51
THE MILLION MAN MARCH	53
I LOVE YOU	55
THOUGHT FOR THE DAY	57
FOR I AM LOVE	59
DETERMINATION	61
SECRET LOVE	63
US	65
WHEN WILL LOVE LEARN TO LOVE	67
THOUGHT FOR THE DAY	69
I AM WHO I AM	71
ALL IS WELL	73
BY MYSELF	75
CONFIDENCE	77
THOUGHT FOR THE DAY	79
JOY	81
HAPPINESS	83
THOUGHT FOR THE DAY	85
TAKE A DEEP BREATH	87
R&B MUSIC OF YESTERDAY	89
DREAMS	91
HISTORY'S LESSON	93
THOUGHT FOR TODAY	95

A SCHOOL MASSACRE	97
SAVE THE BABIES	99
A DEDICATION TO SPECIAL EDUCATION TEACHERS	101
THOUGHT FOR THE DAY	103
SUICIDE	105
THE LOSS OF A MOTHER	107
A LOT MORE LOVE	109
CHERISH THE MOMENTS	111
THOUGHT FOR THE DAY	113
LET IT RAIN	115
AFTER THE STORMS	117
RAIN	119
CONCRETE INVADERS	121
AGE	123
THE FORGOTTEN	125
BLACK LIVES	127
THE ULTIMATE SACRIFICE	129
KAEPERNICK	131
WHEN WILL IT END	133
A BIRD	135
THE TENANT	137
HOLD ONTO LOVE	139
DON'T DRIVE AND DRINK	141
ONE WISH	143
THE MISSING	145
SUN AND MOON	147
PEACE FOR ALL MANKIND	149
THOUGHT FOR THE DAY	151

THOUGHT FOR THE DAY

DON'T BE AFRAID TO OPEN THE DOOR TO YOUR IMAGINATION...
HAPPINESS MAY BE WAITING ON THE OTHER SIDE.

TEACH OUR BABIES

TEACH OUR BABIES TO READ AND WRITE
SO THEY MAY SOAR LIKE EAGLES IN LIFE

TEACH OUR BABIES THE VALUE OF SELF-RESPECT
AND THAT LACK OF SUCH LEADS TO NEGLECT

TEACH THEM THAT PRIDE AND DIGNITY WILL MAKE THEM STAND TALL
AND HATRED AND BIGOTRY ARE WEAPONS OF THE WEAK AND SMALL

TEACH OUR BABIES THAT LOVE OF ONESELF IS NOT TO BE VAIN
IT CAN SOOTHE THE HEART DURING HARDSHIP AND PAIN

TEACH OUR BABIES THERE CAN BE A MESSAGE IN OUR MUSIC
THEN LEAD BY EXAMPLE AND SHOW THEM TO USE IT

TEACH OUR BABIES THAT TRUST IN THEMSELVES THEY MUST NOT LACK
LEST OTHERS WILL USE IT TO HOLD THEM BACK

TEACH THEM THAT GRATITUDE AND LOVE WILL BRING THEM DELIGHT
WHILE HATRED AND VENGENCE WILL KEEP THEM UP AT NIGHT

TEACH THEM THAT NO ONE IS BETTER THAN HE OR SHE
AND WILL NEVER DETERMINE WHAT THEIR FUTURE WILL BE

TEACH THEM THAT THOSE WHO BOAST OF SUPERIORITY
ARE ONLY ATTEMPTING TO MASK THEIR INFERIORITY

TEACH THEM THE LOVE OF ONESELF IS THEIR GREATEST TOOL
BECAUSE IT'S THE ONLY SUBJECT NEVER TAUGHT IN SCHOOL

SEND ME A BOUQUET

IF YOU SHOULD LOVE ME, DON'T SEND A ROSE

NOR SWEET SCENTS OF PERFUME TO TICKLE MY NOSE

DON'T SEND ME CANDY OR DIAMONDS IN RINGS

DON'T SEND ME ANY MATERIAL THINGS

INSTEAD, IF YOU LOVE ME I'M TAKING ALL BIDS
FROM SOMEONE WHO'LL SEND ME A
BOUQUET OF KIDS!

PRETENDING

WHEN THE DAY'S GOTTEN OFF TO A TERRIBLE START
AND SOMEONE HAS BROKEN YOUR POOR LITTLE HEART

DON'T JUST SIT THERE FEELING SAD
PRETEND YOU'RE A LION BIG AND BAD

WHEN YOU'RE TROUBLED AND LIFE'S NO FUN
PRETEND YOU'RE A COUGAR AND RUN AND RUN

WHEN YOU HAVE TO STAY IN YOUR ROOM ALL ALONE
PRETEND YOU'RE A KING ON A ROYAL THRONE

AND IF YOU'RE TOLD, "GO TO BED!"
THINK WHAT YOU'D DO IF YOU WERE RICH INSTEAD

AND ALL THE WHILE THAT YOU'RE PRETENDING
YOUR PRECIOUS LITTLE HEART WILL BE QUICKLY MENDING

ABUSED CHILD

COME CLOSE MY DEAR
LAY YOUR HEAD UPON MY HEART

WE'LL TURN BACK THE TIME
AND WE'LL NEVER HAVE TO PART

CLOSE YOUR LITTLE EYES AND HANG ON TIGHT
JUST CLING TO ME WITH ALL YOUR MIGHT

FROM THE DARKNESS OF NIGHT, TO THE LIGHT OF DAWN
I'LL STAY HERE BESIDE YOU TO KEEP YOU WARM

NO ONE WILL NEVER, EVER LEAVE YOU AGAIN
I'LL SHELTER YOU FROM HARM, I'LL DO ALL I CAN

AND THOUGH YOUR HEART IS FILLED WITH PAIN
THERE IS ONE THING YOU MUST UNDERSTAND

WHAT'S A BURDEN TO ONE, IS ANOTHER'S PLEASURE
AND YOU, MY CHILD, ARE MY GREATEST TREASURE

THOUGHT FOR THE DAY

SMILE. . .IT'S THE GREATEST GIFT OF ALL.

LITTLE ONE
(A GRANDMOTHER'S PRAYER)

CLOSE YOUR EYES LITTLE ONE
YOUR TASK TODAY IS OVER AND DONE

YOU'VE MADE ME SMILE, YOU'VE MADE ME LAUGH
AND ALL THE WHILE YOU'RE GROWING SO FAST

OUR TIME TOGETHER WILL BECOME MEMORIES I KNOW
BUT I'LL HOLD THEM TIGHT AND NEVER LET GO

AND, IF ONE DAY MY TOMORROW NEVER COMES
ALWAYS REMEMBER, I LOVED YOU LITTLE ONE

MY AMAZING SPECIAL NEEDS CHILD

THOUGH YOU MAY BE DIFFERENT FROM OTHERS I SEE

YOU'RE PERFECT, YOU'RE PRECIOUS AND WONDERFUL TO ME

YOU MAY NOT WALK OR YOU MAY NOT TALK

YOUR HANDS MAY NOT LET YOU HOLD A SPOON OR FORK

BUT JUST TO SEE YOUR BEAUTIFUL SMILE

MAKES ALL YOUR IMPERFECTIONS SO WORTH WHILE

THOSE HAPPY SOUNDS THAT SET YOU FREE

ARE OH SO WONDERFUL, LIKE MUSIC TO ME

THERE'S NOTHING ELSE I'D RATHER DO

THAN SPEND MY TIME TAKING CARE OF YOU

AND IF GOD SHOULD SUDDENLY CALL YOU AWAY

I'LL CHERISH OUR MOMENTS TOGETHER EACH DAY

IF OTHERS KNEW YOU LIKE I DO

THEN THEY'D UNDERSTAND WHY I LOVE YOU

MAYBE PULL UP A CHAIR AND STAY A WHILE

THEY'D UNDERSTAND WHY I LOVE MY SPECIAL NEEDS CHILD

A CHILD

I CAN PLAY WITH ANTS AND FLIES
I CAN SEE THROUGH ROSE-COLORED EYES

I CAN PLAY IN MUD AND DIRT
AND NEVER HAVE TO GO TO WORK

I CAN LAY DOWN IN THE GRASS
AND WATCH THE TIME JUST SLOWLY PASS

ALL THESE THINGS I CAN DO
CAUSE I'M A LITTLE CHILD—ARE YOU?

THOUGHT FOR THE DAY

LOVE IS COMPROMISING . . . NOT TYRANNY.

WHAT IS A WOMAN

A WOMAN IS A BEAUTIFUL SOUL TO REVERE
SHE SHOULD NEVER, EVER HAVE TO LIVE IN FEAR

SHE'S THE STRONGEST HUMAN TO GRACE THE EARTH
HER POWER IS SEEN IN HER ABILITY TO GIVE BIRTH

LET US NOT FORGET HER SENSIBILITIES AND INTUITION
MATCHED WITH HER ACHIEVEMENTS AND AMBITION

SHE CAN BE A HOST OF OH SO MANY THINGS
SHE CAN DOMINATE, BE THE KING OF KINGS

LET US NOT FORGET HOW SHE STANDS BY ONE'S SIDE
FORGING A PATH WHILE BEING A GUIDE

A WOMAN IS NOT SIMPLY AN ITEM OF PLEASURE
HER INTELLECTUAL ABILITY IS BEYOND MEASURE

SHE'S ALWAYS THERE, FOR BETTER OR WORSE
THE MOST HEAVENLY CREATURE IN GOD'S UNIVERSE

RESPECT

GIVE HIM YOUR HEART, ENTRUST HIM WITH YOUR SOUL
WORRY NOT ABOUT DECEIT OR WHO'S IN CONTROL

THE LOVE OF YOURSELF WILL NOT STEER YOU WRONG
BUT LEND TO YOU GUIDANCE AND KEEP YOU STRONG

FEAR NOT THAT YOUR LOVE WILL BE FORSAKEN
TAKE LOVE SLOW, CHART THE PATH TO BE TAKEN

EARN HIS RESPECT BY RETURNING HIM THE SAME
KEEP SOME LOVE FOR YOURSELF WITHOUT BEING VAIN

LET HIM BE THE MAN HE STRIVES TO BE
SHOW HIM THE WAY WHEN HE CANNOT SEE

STAND BY HIS SIDE WHEN HE NEEDS A FRIEND
SHOW HIM YOU'LL BE THERE UNTIL THE END

AND IF YOU FEEL HIS LOVE STARTING TO FADE
RESPECT HIM BY TELLING HIM, PLAY NO CHARADE

TAKE LIFE STRAIGHT, NO GAMES OF THE HEART
WHEN RESPECT IS LOST, IT'S TIME TO PART

ACCEPT YOUR PAIN AS A LESSON LEARNED
RETAIN THE RESPECT THAT YOU HAVE EARNED

AND AS YOU WATCH HIM EXIT YOUR HEART
YOU'LL KNOW THAT YOU TRIED FROM THE VERY START

SHOWER HIM WITH LOVE AND GIVE HIM RESPECT
AND WHEN IT'S ALL OVER, YOU'LL HAVE NO REGRET

AFTER THE BREAKUP

YOU'RE ANGRY BECAUSE YOU'RE TOLD THE LOVE MUST END
AND YOU COULD NEVER BE MORE THAN A FRIEND

YOU FEEL YOUR HEART WILL NEVER MEND
YOU FEEL BETRAYED, YOU WANT REVENGE

YOU'RE TOO EMOTIONAL, IN A FIT OF RAGE
YOU'RE LIKE A BOMB, LIKE AN ANIMAL IN A CAGE

BUT WHERE IS YOUR PRIDE, YOUR LOVE OF SELF
WHY TORMENT YOURSELF FOR SOMEONE ELSE

BE STILL, BE PATIENT AND CALM THE HEART
GET CONTROL OF YOURSELF, THAT'S THE PLACE TO START

REMEMBER, YOU HAVE A LIFE THAT'S YOURS TO LIVE
AND SO MUCH MORE LOVE INSIDE TO GIVE

SISTERS

SISTERS! WHY IS IT WE HAVE COME TO BE
RECEPTIVE OF THE BEHAVIORS ASSIGNED TO YOU AND ME

ANGRY, DEFENSIVE, EVIL AND CRUDE
DISREPECTING EACH OTHER AND JUST PLAIN RUDE

WE PASS ON THE STREET AND I GIVE YOU A SMILE
YOU REFUSE TO RECIPROCATE, WITH A LOOK THAT'S VILE

I'M WITH YOU MY SISTERS, I MEAN YOU NO HARM
WE SHOULD BE PROUD OF EACH OTHER'S BEAUTY AND CHARM

WE'RE IN THIS TOGETHER, WE'RE NOT AT WAR
LIFE IS WONDERFUL, WE'VE COME SO FAR

NOW LET'S CALL A TRUCE, LET'S TRY TO BE KIND
COULD BE I'M THE BEST FRIEND YOU'LL EVER FIND

(PEACE AND LOVE TO ALL MY SISTERS)

DOMESTIC ABUSE

YOU GREW UP BEAUTIFUL, YOUNG AND SMART
WITH SO MUCH LOVE DEEP IN YOUR HEART

SOMETIMES YOU'LL WONDER IF TRUE LOVE WILL EVER COME
AND, IF NOT, YOU'LL QUESTION WHAT YOU HAVE DONE

YOU'LL NEVER SEARCH FOR LOVE INSIDE YOURSELF
INSTEAD, YOU'LL YEARN FOR IT FROM SOMEONE ELSE

NOT KNOWING THAT YOU ARE GOD'S GREATEST GIFT
NO AMOUNT OF PRAISE WILL GIVE YOUR SPIRIT A LIFT

NOT KNOWING YOUR WORTH WILL BE YOUR BIGGEST DOWNFALL
IT 'LL MAKE YOU FEEL HOPELESS AND VERY VULNERABLE

BUT THE GREATEST THING THAT YOU CAN DO
IS SIMPLY LEARN TO LOVE YOU FOR YOU

NEVER BEG FOR LOVE FROM SOMEONE ELSE
YOU MAY WIND UP FINDING YOU'RE FAILING YOURSELF

AS TIME GOES ON, YOU MAY MEET A MAN
WHO'S SEEMINGLY YOUR BIGGEST FAN

HIS WAY OF LOVING YOU WILL BE TO SHOW NEGLECT
CHEATING, FIGHTING AND DISRESPECT

ACCEPT NO APOLOGY FOR HIS DOMESTIC ABUSE
HIS HOLLOW APOLOGY SERVES NO USE

KNOW WHO YOU ARE, IT'S NEVER TOO LATE
YOU'RE WONDERFUL, YOU'RE PRICELESS, GREATER THAN GREAT

HOLD YOUR HEAD HIGH AND EXIT THE DOOR
THEN TELL YOURSELF, NEVER MORE!

(DEDICATED TO EACH AND EVERY VICTIM OF DOMESTIC ABUSE)

JUST LEAVE

IF YOU FEEL YOUR LIFE'S IN TROUBLE
GET OUT FAST, ON THE DOUBLE

DON'T WAIT AROUND, DON'T HESITATE
ONE MORE SECOND COULD BE TOO LATE

DON'T WAIT AROUND FOR DANGER TO COME
PACK YOUR THINGS AND RUN AND RUN

TELL SOMEONE, GET ON THE PHONE
THE LIFE YOU SAVE COULD BE YOUR OWN

(DOMESTIC VIOLENCE IS REAL)

IT'S JUST ME! (AND I LOVE IT)

I PASS THE MIRROR AND I STOP AND STARE
THEN REMIND MYSELF, "IT'S JUST ME WITHOUT HAIR"

SOMETIMES I QUESTION WHY IT HAPPENED TO ME
THEN I ANSWER, "BECAUSE HAIR DOESN'T DEFINE BEAUTY"

I USED TO CURSE MY ILLNESS, SOMETIMES I'D BREAK DOWN AND CRY
THERE WERE EVEN TIMES I THOUGHT THAT I WOULD DIE

WHILE AT FIRST I CRIED AND SLUMPED INTO DEPRESSION
I LATER REALIZED NATURAL BEAUTY WAS AN AWESOME EXPESSION

THOUGH FEW SEEMED TO NOTICE AND SOME WOULD DISCRETELY STARE
MANY OTHERS WOOED ME SAYING, "YOU'RE BEAUTIFUL WITHOUT HAIR"

IT'S BECOME QUITE NATURAL FROM MEN AND WOMEN I MEET
THE GLOWING COMPLIMENTS I GET WHILE PASSING ON THE STREET

NOW, THERE'S A SMILE ON MY FACE AND I HAVE TO ADMIT
I'M PROUD TO SAY, "IT'S JUST ME AND I LOVE IT!"

(DEDICATED TO ALL WOMEN WHO PROUDLY EMBRACE NATURAL BEAUTY)

JUST THAT KIND OF GIRL

I CLIMBED A MOUNTAIN THAT REACHED THE SKY
THE CLOUDS WERE SHOCKED TO SEE IT WAS I

THEY PARTED AND MADE A PATH FOR ME
AS THEY ASKED ME HOW IT CAME TO BE

THAT I COULD RISE ABOVE THEM ALL
I, WHO WAS EVER SO TINY AND SMALL

I SHOT THEM A GRIN AND PAUSED A WHILE
THEN SAID TO THEM, "THAT'S JUST MY STYLE"

I WILL ALWAYS RISE ABOVE MY WORLD
YOU SEE I AM JUST THAT KIND OF GIRL

(DEDICATED TO ALL FEMALES YOUNG AND OLD. NEVER STOP RISING.)

THOUGHT FOR THE DAY

MY MAN? YOUR MAN? GOD'S MAN!

FOREVER YOU

STRONG, DARK, HANDSOME, WHAT A SIGHT TO BEHOLD
MORE PRECIOUS TO ME THAN DIAMONDS AND GOLD

TALLER THAN A MOUNTAIN, SO STATUESQUE
BETTER THAN BETTER, SIMPLY THE BEST

LIKE A SMOOTH LIQUOR, SO UTTERLY PLEASING
THE RHYTHM IN YOUR STRIDE, SEDUCTIVE AND TEASING

SMOLDERING FIRES IN YOUR AFTERMATH
THE BURNING TRAIL OF YOUR CHOSEN PATH

THE TASTE OF DESIRE, THE WARMTH OF ADORATION
VERY MUCH IN DEMAND FOR MERE CONVERSATION

INCREDIBLE STRENGTH, ENDURABLE HEARTS
SO GENUINELY GIFTED WITH THE FINEST OF PARTS

OH YOU GORGEOUS BLACK MEN

I DON'T KNOW WHAT YOU DO

BUT WHATEVER IT IS...

STAY FOREVER YOU

LOVE IS ON THE WAY

HOLD ON MY BROTHERS AND DON'T LOSE SIGHT
I SEE YOU, I HEAR YOU, I UNDERSTAND YOUR FIGHT

WHETHER PLAYING A SPORT OR DRIVING A CAR
THERE ARE MANY WHO REFUSE TO ACCEPT WHO YOU ARE

YOU'RE GORGEOUS, YOU'RE BRILLIANT, YOU'RE A BEAUTY TO BEHOLD
BUT YOUR INFLUENCE ON THE WORLD WILL NEVER BE TOLD

FROM THE NBA TO THE SUPER BOWL
EVERYTHING YOU TOUCH TURNS TO GOLD

FROM THE WAY YOU DANCE, TO THE WAY YOU RAP
YOUR STYLE IS IMITATED ALL OVER THE MAP

BE YOU AN EVERYDAY CITIZEN OR A SUPER STAR
YOU'LL STILL FACE RACISM NO MATTER WHO YOU ARE

FROM THE BOY NEXT DOOR, TO THE PRESIDENT
YOU'RE STILL MET WITH ENVY AND DISSENT

BUT FIGHT THOUGHTS OF HOPELESSNESS AND STAY IN THE GAME
KNOW IT'S NOT OVER TILL HE CALLS YOUR NAME

THE DARKER THE FLESH, THE DEEPER I LOVE

I SAVOR THE TASTE OF THAT PECAN-BROWN KISS
DRIPPING WITH PASSION FROM THOSE SOFT, FULL LIPS

I YEARN TO BE HELD IN THOSE BROWN-SKINNED ARMS
SO TENDER, SO WARM, AND YET SO STRONG

OH YES, THOSE WOMEN THEY KNOW WHAT I'VE GOT
TRADE FOR THEIR MEN, "NO THANKS, I'D RATHER NOT"

I'M SO DARN SATISFIED WITH MY MAN OF COLOR
WOULDN'T TRADE HIM FOR THE WORLD, NOT FOR ANOTHER

GOLDENROD, PECAN, RUST, MAHOGANY, AND COAL
THE DARKER THE COLOR, THE RICHER THE GOLD

GUESS YOU CAN SAY THAT I'VE GOT IT BAD
DON'T KNOW NOTHIN' ELSE, HE'S ALL I'VE EVER HAD

AND IF I HAD TO DO IT ALL AGAIN
I'D SELL MY SOUL FOR ANOTHER BLACK MAN

HIS STYLE, HIS PRIDE, ONE SO DIVINE
JUST CAN'T HELP BUT MAKE HIM MINE

THAT TIGHT BROWN SKIN THAT FITS LIKE A GLOVE
THE DARKER THE FLESH, THE DEEPER I LOVE

PEANUT BUTTER MAN

SMOOTH, BROWN, CREAMY AND SO SINFULLY SWEET
FROM THE TOP OF HIS HEAD TO THE BOTTOM OF HIS FEET

MY PEANUT BUTTER MAN, SO SOOTHING AND ENTICING
WITH GUMDROP EYES THAT LOOK SO INVITING

SO VELVETY RICH WITH THE SOFTEST TOUCH
THAT SATIN BROWN SKIN THAT I LOVE SO MUCH

I'LL HAVE ONE PIECE NOW AND WHEN I'M THROUGH
I'LL HAVE THE OTHER IN AN HOUR OR TWO

SMACK MY LIPS AND CLOSE MY EYES
AS I SLOWLY RELISH MY PEANUT BUTTER SURPRISE

I'LL TAKE ME A NAP, THEN RISE AGAIN
AND HAVE ANOTHER PIECE OF MY PEANUT BUTTER MAN

THE THIEF

HE WALKED IN THE DOOR WITH THAT LOOK IN HIS EYES
I DROPPED MY GUARD, I HAD NO DISGUISE

THAT SWAY OF CONFIDENCE WITH A DASH OF VANITY
NEARLY DROVE ME STRAIGHT TO THE BRINK OF INSANITY

HIS BODY SWAYED, SO GRACEFUL AND FLUENT
MY DEFENSE WAS GONE, I WAS EMOTIONALLY RUINED

THAT MAGNIFICENT BODY WITH CHOCOLATE BROWN SKIN
HE SHOT ME A LOOK WITH A WICKED GRIN

AS HE CROSSED THE FLOOR, I BRACED FOR FEAR
MY POUNDING HEART HE MIGHT HEAR

HE PARTED HIS LIPS AND BEGAN TO SPEAK
MY STOMACH CHURNED AND MY LEGS GOT WEAK

I COULD NOT TALK, NO WORDS COULD I FIND
HE WAS UNDOUBTEDLY COMMITTING A CRIME

BUT I, TOO, WAS GUILTY FROM THE VERY START
I WANTED THIS THIEF TO STEAL MY HEART

WHERE ARE THE GOOD BLACK MEN

I RECENTLY HEARD THAT QUESTION ASKED
AND AT THAT MOMENT I HAD A FLASH

GIRLS MUST WE ALWAYS LOOK SO HARD
FOR WHAT COULD BE IN OUR OWN BACKYARD

SEE THERE'S A PRACTICE SOMEONE DISCOVERED
CALLED JUDGING A BOOK BY ITS COVER

WE TEND TO SEE BUT ARE SO BLIND
BECAUSE OF WHAT IS IN OUR MINDS

TO GIVE AN EXAMPLE, I'LL CLUE YOU IN
TO WHY SOME OF US FEEL THERE ARE NO MEN

YOU LOOK OUT YOUR WINDOW AND THERE'S A MAN
BUT YOU SAY, "NO WAY, HE'S MY GARBAGE MAN"

YOU FROWN UP YOUR FACE AS HE WAVES HELLO
YOU THROW UP YOUR HEAD AS HIGH AS IT'LL GO

BUT DEEP INSIDE YOU'RE FRUSTRATED AND ALONE
YOU HAVE A HOUSE, BUT IT'S HARDLY A HOME

YOU'VE SET YOUR STANDARDS FOR WHAT HE MUST BE
AND NOW IT'S CAUSING YOU MISERY

YOU SAY, "HE'S NOT THIS" OR "HE DOESN'T HAVE"
BUT TO WHAT STANDARDS DO YOU, YOURSELF, COMPARE

YOU MIGHT WANT A MAN IN A SUIT AND TIE
WHO COULD BE HOOKED ON A RICH MAN'S HIGH

WHETHER RICH OR POOR, WHETHER SUIT AND TIE
THEY ALL ARE MEN, THEY CAN ALL MAKE YOU CRY

GIRLS IT'S TIME TO TAKE A LOOK INSIDE
CUT THE PHONY CRAP, CUT THE FOOLISH PRIDE

LET'S NOT JUDGE OUR MEN BY THE ACTS OF OTHERS
LET'S NOT JUDGE OUR BOOKS SIMPLY BY THE COVERS

AND REMEMBER, YOUR SEARCH NEED NOT BE SO HARD
IT MAY BE NO FURTHER THAN YOUR OWN BACK YARD

JOB WELL DONE
(A SINGLE FATHER)

HE WAS A SINGLE FATHER LIVING ALONE
RAISING HIS KIDS IN A SINGLE-PARENT HOME

HE NEVER THOUGHT TWICE ABOUT WHAT TO DO
HE ONLY KNEW THAT THEY WOULD GET THROUGH

HE HELD ON TO FAITH WHEN TIMES WERE BAD
AND DID THE BEST WITH WHAT THEY HAD

HE NURTURED THEM THROUGH COLDS AND FLU
SOMETIMES WITHOUT EVEN HAVING A CLUE

FINDING A DAY JOB WAS HIS GREATEST GIFT
HE'D NEVER LEAVE THEM TO WORK NIGHT SHIFT

THROUGH IT ALL, HE NEVER LEFT THEIR SIDE
HE WATCHED THEM GROW UP BEAMING WITH PRIDE

WHAT MADE HIM DIFFERENT, WHAT SET HIM APART
WAS THE LOVE FOR HIS KIDS THAT HE HAD IN HIS HEART

TODAY WHEN HE LOOKS AT WHO THEY'VE BECOME
HE THINKS TO HIMSELF, "MY JOB WAS WELL DONE"

(DEDICATED TO ALL SINGLE FATHERS)

THE MILLION MAN MARCH (THE HIDDEN HISTORY)

WHAT A BEAUTIFUL SIGHT FOR THE EYES TO BEHOLD
YET THIS IS A STORY THAT'S SELDOM TOLD

OVER ONE MILLION MALES STANDING SHOULDER TO SHOULDER
LITTLE BOYS, TEENAGERS AND MANY MEN MUCH OLDER

SUCH BEAUTY AND MAGNIFICENCE ALL IN ONE PLACE
WITH A LOOK OF PEACE ON EACH AND EVERY FACE

ALLAH/GOD LOOKED DOWN FROM THE HEAVENS ABOVE
SHOWERING EACH MALE'S FACE WITH A LOOK OF LOVE

OH ALLAH/GOD I GIVE PRAISE TO YOU
FOR THIS WAS SOMETHING ONLY YOU COULD DO

A CALL TO ACTION, A CALL TO PRAYER
NOT A SOUL WAS HARMED, NOT EVEN A HAIR

FOR ONE MAN HAD DONE WHAT NO LEADER CAN
DEVOTING HIS LIFE TO SAVING THE BLACK MAN

MORE THAN ONE MILLION MEN ON THE WASHINGTON MALL
THEY CAME IN ANSWER TO ONE MAN'S CALL

THEY POSED NO THREAT, THEY POSED NO DANGER
PEACE AND LOVE FILLED THEIR HEARTS, NO HATRED, NO ANGER

WHY THIS DATE IS NOT COMMEMORATED IS A MYSTERY
IT SEEMS TO BE A PART OF OUR "HIDDEN HISTORY"

EACH DAY I GIVE THANKS TO THE HONORABLE MINISTER FARRAKHAN

IN RETURN FOR HIS GRACE, I HUMBLY SAY
"WA ALAIKUM SALAAM"

I LOVE YOU

I LOVE YOU JUST FOR YOU
THAT'S WHAT ALLAH/GOD WANTS ME TO DO

DOESN'T MATTER IF YOU'RE FAT OR THIN
DOESN'T MATTER THE COLOR OF YOUR SKIN

DOESN'T MATTER IF YOU HAVE HAIR OR BALD
DOESN'T MATTER IF YOU'RE SHORT OR TALL

WHY SHOULD LOVE COME WITH A CONDITION
WHEN SOME OF US ARE IN NO POSITION

TO COMMENT ON THE WAY THAT OTHERS LOOK
WHEN WE WEREN'T CUT FROM A PERFECT BOOK

DOESN'T MATTER IF YOU HAVE LINES IN YOUR FACE
THAT'S WHAT HAPPENS IN THE HUMAN RACE

DOESN'T MATTER IF YOUR FEET ARE BIG OR SMALL
DOESN'T MATTER IF YOU HAVE NO FEET AT ALL

LOVE DOESN'T CARE WHAT'S ON THE OUTSIDE
LOVE LOOKS DEEP INTO YOU INSIDE

DOESN'T MATTER IF YOU HAVE A YACHT THAT SAILS
DOESN'T MATTER IF YOU'VE BEEN TO JAIL

LOVE DOESN'T CARE ABOUT YOUR FAITH
DOESN'T MATTER WHO YOU MARRY OR DATE

LOVE HAS NO TIME FOR WASTED PREFERENCE
LOVE LOVES ALL, IT REQUIRES NO REFERENCE

LOVE SEES BEAUTY BUT BOWS NOT TO IT
LOVE SEES US ALL AS A PERFECT FIT

LOVE LOVES ALL AND PASSES NO JUDGEMENT
LOVE SEES SUCH AS SELF-SERVING AND REPUGNANT

SO LET US LOVE OUR SISTERS AND BROTHERS
AND NOT COMPARE THEM TO OURSELVES OR OTHERS

JUST BE YOURSELF NOTHING FURTHER TO DO
CAUSE NO MATTER WHAT, I LOVE YOU FOR YOU

THOUGHT FOR THE DAY

TRUE LOVE CAN NEVER BE CONQUERED.

FOR I AM LOVE

THOUGH YOU MAY NOT KNOW IT, THOUGH YOU MAY NOT CARE
I'M ALWAYS AROUND, I'M ALWAYS THERE

I'M EVERY TEAR YOU CRY
I'M EVERY HELLO AND GOODBYE

I'M EVERY PAIN YOU FEEL WHEN YOUR POOR HEART ACHES
I'M EVERY BAD HABIT YOU CAN'T SEEM TO BREAK

I'M EVERY SHIVER YOU HAVE WHEN YOUR BODY IS CHILLED
I'M YOUR SECRET FANTASY, I'M YOUR EVERY THRILL

I'M YOUR LIFE, I'M YOUR BREATH, I'M A PART OF YOU NOW
I'LL BE WITH YOU ALWAYS, NO MATTER WHAT NO MATTER HOW

I'LL STAY WITH YOU FOREVER, WE'LL NEVER BE APART
I'M YOUR EVERY EMOTION, I'M DEEP IN YOUR HEART

AND IF GOD SHOULD CALL YOU TO THE HEAVENS ABOVE
I'LL BE THERE WAITING—FOR I AM LOVE

DETERMINATION

THOUGH YOU'VE TORN MY HEART APART...
I WILL NOT CRY

YOU'VE SHAKEN MY FAITH IN MANKIND, BUT...
I WILL NOT CRY

MY YESTERDAYS ARE FILLED WITH SORROW
AND MY TOMORROWS ARE UNCERTAIN, BUT...
I WILL NOT CRY

I WATCHED AS MY GRIEF TURNED TO PITY
THEN ANGER AND AGAIN TO LOVE, BUT...
I WILL NOT CRY

EACH DAY I STRUGGLE WITH MY EMOTIONS
STILL, I'M DETERMINED TO GO FORWARD

I BEAR NO HATRED, NO ANGER, MY FEELINGS ARE
INNOCUOUS

I'VE LEARNED TO ACCEPT DECEIT AT FACE VALUE
BECAUSE I KNOW THAT I'M WORTHY OF MORE

I'VE LEARNED TO SHUN WHAT HURTS AND TO GRASP WHAT
HEALS

AND I KNOW THAT DETERMINATION WILL HEAL MY SOUL

SECRET LOVE

TO EXPRESS MY LOVE FOR YOU WOULD GO BEYOND
THE GREATEST DEPTH OF SILENCE
WORDS CANNOT EXPLAIN...

MY MIND WANDERS, REACHES OUT, TOUCHES AND EXPLORES
THE SANITY OF MY BEING
WORDS CANNOT EXPLAIN...

WHY ME, WHY YOU, WHY LOVE?

WORDS CANNOT EXPLAIN...

TO HAVE LOVED SO LONG AND YET REMAINED IN SILENCE
ANTICIPATING HAPPINESS AND FEARING HURT, WHY?
WORDS CANNOT EXPLAIN...

AND YET I HAVE VOWED TO LOVE YOU ETERNALLY, WHY?
I CANNOT EXPLAIN...

US

IT'S AMAZING WHAT WE'VE ACCOMPLISHED IN SO LITTLE TIME
THE TIES THAT BIND US CAN NEVER BE BROKEN
ONLY BE STRENGTHENED TO MAKE US STRONGER

WE HAVE BETWEEN US A MAGIC NO ONE COULD EVER IMAGINE
TOGETHER WE CAN BRING FORTH THE RAIN OR SPRINKLE A RAY OF SUNSHINE
THAT'S THE POWER WE POSSESS

SO MANY MEMORIES THAT WILL LINGER AFTER WHAT WE HAVE HAS VANISHED
BECAUSE IN OUR HEARTS WE WILL ALWAYS LOVE ON
LONG AFTER WHAT WE HAVE HAS COME TO PASS

AND WE KNOW THAT AS LONG AS WE EXIST, WE CAN NEVER REPLACE EACH OTHER

SURELY, OUR LIVES WILL GO ON, BUT THERE WILL NEVER BE ANOTHER YOU
AND THERE WILL NEVER BE ANOTHER ME

WHEN WILL LOVE LEARN TO LOVE

I AM LOVE, YOU ARE LOVE
BUT WHY IS THERE ALWAYS PUSH AND SHOVE

I LOVE YOU JUST FOR YOU
NOT FOR WHAT YOU HAVE OR DO

IF LOVE COMES FROM ALLAH/GOD ABOVE
WHY CAN'T WE JUST LEARN TO LOVE

WHY CAN'T YOU LOVE ME FOR ME
NOT FOR WHAT YOU THINK OF ME

IF I AM LOVE AND YOU ARE LOVE
WHY CAN'T WE JUST LEARN TO LOVE

WHY DON'T WE STOP WITH ALL THE PUSH AND SHOVE
AND LET US ALL JUST LEARN TO LOVE

THOUGHT FOR THE DAY

EVERY EMOTION HAS A PURPOSE.

I AM WHO I AM

KNOW THAT YOU ARE A WINNER

LET NO ONE OR NOTHING DETER YOU

STAY ON YOUR PATH AND MAKE NO EXCUSES

FOLLOW THE ROAD

KNOW WHO YOU ARE AND BE PROUD OF WHO YOU ARE

TREAT OTHERS WITH KINDNESS

BUT NEVER BEG FOR ACCEPTANCE

CONTINUE TO FACE LIFE AND ALL ITS CHALLENGES WITH A
SMILE AND
DETERMINATION

AND ALWAYS SAY...

I AM WHO I AM

ALL IS WELL

WE SOMETIMES INTENTIONALLY OR UNINTENTIONALLY COME UPON LONG, UNFAMILIAR
ROADS IN THE PATH OF LIFE

OFTENTIMES, WE DON'T KNOW WHERE THE ROADS LEAD OR IF WE'RE TRESPASSING
ON THE THREAD OF LIFE

WITHOUT KNOWING, WE CAN ONLY LIVE IN FEAR OF WHAT MIGHT BE
OR FORGE AHEAD AND BELIEVE THAT ALL WILL AND CAN ONLY BE WELL

WHETHER IN DANGER OR SAFETY, WE MUST KNOW THAT THE ROAD WE TOOK
WAS NOT IN VAIN

WE MUST LOOK AT DEFEAT AND SEE SUCCESS—SUCCESS IN HAVING KNOWN DEFEAT

WE MUST LOOK AT FEAR AND SEE SAFTY—SAFETY IN KNOWING THAT BOUNDARIES EXIST

WE MUST LOOK AT SADNESS AND SEE JOY—JOY IN KNOWING THINGS CAN GET BETTER

WE MUST LOOK AT WHAT APPEARS TO BE THE END AND SEE A BEGINNING—A BEGINNING OF A WONDERFUL, NEW JOURNEY

WHEN WE COMBINE THEM, ONLY THEN CAN WE EMPLOY THEM AS THE RICH OPPORTUNITY THEY PRESENT

TO INTENTIONALLY OR UNINTENTIONALLY EMBARK UPON OUR NEXT PATH IN LIFE

BELIEVING THAT ALL IS AND CAN ONLY BE...WELL

BY MYSELF

THRASHING, PULLING, PUSHING, AND KICKING I WAS THRUST
INTO THIS WORLD

MINDFUL OF MY SURROUNDINGS, I WENT ABOUT MY
BUSINESS ESCAPING INTO MY SOLITUDE

GROWING OLDER, I LEARNED TO RESPECT THE INNER PEACE
THAT SELF-CONFIDENCE AND SELF-LOVE CAN BRING

DAY BY DAY, I WALLOW IN THE DELIGHT OF THE JOY OF LIFE
LIFE AS IT IS NOW MINE AND LIFE AS IT WILL BE MINE

AND WITH EACH MOMENT OF SILENCE I'M CONTENT

CONFIDENCE

FEELING DOUBT

I WALKED ALONG A DESPAIRING TRAIL

FAILING TO LOOK WHERE I WAS GOING

I TRIPPED

I STUMBLED BUT NEVER FELL

AND TO MY SURPRISE

I REGAINED MY BALANCE

IT BECAME EVEN STEADIER THAN EVER BEFORE

IT WAS THEN THAT I REALIZED

THAT I HAD STUMBLED UPON CONFIDENCE

THOUGHT FOR THE DAY

POSITIVE THOUGHTS GENERATE SMILES.

JOY

KNOW THAT JOY DOESN'T ONLY COME WITH MATERIAL GIFTS
THOUGH FOR THE MOMENT, THEY MAY GIVE YOU A LIFT

KNOW THAT TRUE JOY CAN ONLY COME FROM WITHIN
AND ONCE YOU HAVE FOUND IT, IT WILL NEVER EVER END

HAPPINESS

HAPPINESS DANCES ACROSS MY SOUL AND TICKLES MY ENTIRE BEING

IT CAUSES ME TO SMILE AT STRANGERS AND URGES ME TO HAVE PATIENCE

IT ENCOURAGES ME TO GIVE TO THE LESS FORTUNATE

AND APPRECIATE THOSE WHO ARE WILLING TO SHARE

IT GIVES ME COMPASSION AND COMPELS ME TO WISH OTHERS WELL

IT FILLS ME WITH GRATITUDE AND APPRECIATION FOR LIFE

IT GIVES ME THE WISDOM TO UNDERSTAND BAD AND APPRECIATE GOOD

IT GIVES ME CALM WHEN ALL IS RAGING AROUND ME

IT SLOWS MY PULSE AND HEALS MY RACING HEART

YES, HAPPINESS WILL CARRY ME ON ITS WINGS TO GREATER HEALTH AND A FULFILLING LIFE

THOUGHT FOR THE DAY

EVERY SECOND IS A BEGINNING — IT'S A CHANCE TO START OVER.

TAKE A DEEP BREATH

TAKE A DEEP BREATH AND FOCUS ON YOURSELF
LOVE OF ONESELF PROMOTES GOOD HEALTH

POLITICS AND NEWS MAKE FOR A GOOD CHAT
BUT IN REALITY, IT'S JUST THAT

DON'T LET BAD THOUGHTS RUN RAMPANT IN YOUR HEAD
WHILE POLITICIANS AND NEWS ANCHORS ARE ASLEEP IN BED

WHILE THEY HAVE THEIR JOBS TO DO
YOU DO YOURS BY TAKING CARE OF YOU

SLEEPLESS NIGHTS, FRUSTRATION AND ANXIETY
OFTEN RESULT FROM WHAT WE HEAR AND SEE

LISTEN FOR A WHILE, BUT THEN TAKE A DEEP BREATH
IT'S THE BEST WAY TO TAKE CARE OF ONESELF

AFTER YOU'VE TAKEN A LONG, DEEP BREATH
THEN MARVEL AT HOW MUCH YOU LOVE YOURSELF

R&B MUSIC OF YESTERDAY

I LOVE THE MUSIC OF YESTERDAY
I LOVE THE LYRICS THEY USED TO SAY

NO CURSING, NO VIOLENCE, NO DISRESPECT
JUST WORDS OF LOVE AND DEEP REGRET

THE MEN KNEW HOW TO BEG BACK THEN
THEY'D ALMOST CRY JUST TO GET BACK IN

THEY SANG ABOUT LOVE AND BEING IN LOVE
THEY EVEN MOANED AND CALLED ON GOD ABOVE

THE WOMEN SANG OF LOVE, HURT AND REJECTION
BUT MOST OF ALL, THEY SANG OF TRUE AFFECTION

THE MUSIC TAUGHT US RIGHT FROM WRONG
THERE WAS A MESSAGE IN EVERY SONG

NO MATTER WHAT I HEAR TODAY
I STILL LONG FOR THE MUSIC OF "YESTERDAY"

(DEDICATED TO ALL R&B ARTISTS OF "YESTERDAY")

DREAMS

HATRED IS DEAD

CAST INTO THE HOTTEST FLAMES OF FIRE

EVIL HAS ERODED TO BE NO MORE

PREJUDICE IS MERELY A BELIEF OF THE PAST

NOW THAT WE'VE WALLOWED IN THE SANDS OF OUR IMAGINATIONS

WELCOME BACK TO REALITY

HISTORY'S LESSON

HAS TIME TAUGHT US NOT TO RESPECT OUT OF FEAR?

BUT TO QUESTION THAT RESPECT WHEN INJUSTICE SEEMS NEAR

HAS TIME TAUGHT US NOT TO OFFER THE OTHER CHEEK?

NOT TO COWER, NOT TO KNEEL AT ANY MAN'S FEET?

HAS TIME TAUGHT US NOT THAT WE'LL NEED OUR OWN

WHEN THEY'VE USED US AND DIVIDED US AND LEFT US ALONE?

YES, TIME HAS TAUGHT US, BUT SOME OF US SEEM NOT TO LEARN

TO CONTINUE THE STRUGGLE FOR WHAT WE'VE EARNED

TO HOLD OUR HEADS HIGH AND REMAIN FOREVER PROUD

TO BE TRUE TO OUR COLOR AND SING OUR PRAISE LOUD

TO KNOW THAT INSIDE US IS A WILL TO BE

THAT WILL KEEP US GOING FOR ALL ETERNITY

THOUGHT FOR TODAY

BE GRATEFUL FOR TODAY DID NOT HAVE TO BE.

A SCHOOL MASSACRE

TODAY THERE WERE STUDENTS ON MY TELEVISION SCREEN
WITH A MESSAGE TO THE ESTABLISHMENT LIKE I'VE NEVER SEEN

THEIR WORDS RANG VERY LOUD AND CLEAR
THEY TOLD THE POLITICIANS TO LISTEN HERE

WE'RE SICK AND TIRED OF YOUR LACK OF ACTION
YOUR JOB PERFORMANCE IS BELOW SATISFACTION

IF YOU WANT TO KEEP YOUR JOB TODAY
YOU'D BETTER WORK TO EARN YOUR PAY

THEY SPOKE WITH SO MUCH COURAGE AND CONVICTION
I COULD TELL THOSE KIDS WERE ON A MISSION

THEY TOLD OF A MASSACRE THAT HAPPENED AT THEIR SCHOOL
NOW WAS NOT THE TIME TO KEEP THEIR COOL

THEY WARNED, THEY PROMISED, THEY EVEN SEEMED TO MAKE A BET
THAT THIS WOULD BE THE LAST SCHOOL KILLING YET

THESE KIDS RANG A BLATANT, CHILLING ALARM
THEY'D FIGHT TO ENSURE NO OTHERS WERE HARMED

(TRIBUTE TO THE STUDENTS OF MARJORIE STONEMAN DOUGLAS HIGH)

SAVE THE BABIES

AGAIN, THE WORLD WITNESSED SOMETHING VICIOUS AND CRUEL
CHILDREN BEING MURDERED WHILE AT SCHOOL

THEIR PARENTS DROPPED THEM OFF TO LEARN AND HAVE FUN
NOT KNOWING THEY'D BE MURDERED BY A MAN WITH A GUN

EVERYDAY OUR CHILDREN ARE SUBJECTED TO DANGER
BECAUSE WE LIVE IN A SOCIETY FULL OF SICKNESS AND ANGER

WE MUST ADMIT THERE IS NOTHING AS VILE
AS TAKING THE LIFE OF AN INNOCENT CHILD

MY HEART CRIES OUT FOR THE CHILDREN THAT WERE LOST
SCHOOL SHOOTINGS MUST STOP NO MATTER THE COST

(DEDICATED TO THE FAMILIES OF THE DECEASED STUDENTS OF ROBB ELEMENTARY, UVALDE TEXAS)

A DEDICATION TO SPECIAL EDUCATION TEACHERS

YOU CHOSE A PROFESSION THAT SHOWS YOU CARE
YOU TAKE THE TIME WHEN OTHERS WOULDN'T DARE

THE TIME YOU TAKE HAS PROVEN TO HELP SOMEONE
TO BE WHO OTHERS DOUBTED THEY'D EVER BECOME

YOU JOB IS NOT EASY, IT CAN BE EXTREMELY TOUGH
FOR ALL THAT YOU DO, THE PAY IS NEVER EOUGH

BUT KNOW THAT YOU'RE RESPECTED AND TRULY ADMIRED
YOU'RE SOME OF THE BEST THAT'S EVER BEEN HIRED

EMPLOYEES LIKE YOU ARE NOT EASY TO FIND
YOUR PATIENCE AND COMPASSION IS ONE OF A KIND

IF NO ONE HAS RECENTLY SAID THIS TO YOU
WE APPRECIATE YOU AND ALL THAT YOU DO

THOUGHT FOR THE DAY

SAVE THE MIND AND SAVE THE BODY.

SUICIDE

THEIR SILENT CRIES WENT OUT FOR HELP
FOR MANY, MANY, NIGHTS THEY HAD NOT SLEPT

IT WAS BECAUSE OF SOMETHING THEY HAD EXPERIENCED
PERHAPS AN UNCOMFORTABLE OR HORRIFYING OCCURRENCE

A HEINOUS ACT THAT WAS NOT COOL
IT HAPPENED TO A STUDENT WHILE AT SCHOOL

A DEMANDING BOSS, JUST BEING A JERK
HARRASSING THEM EACH DAY AT WORK

A SUDDEN ALARMING MEDICAL DIAGNOSIS
AN UNKNOWN ILLNESS OR A CASE OF PSYCHOSIS

A ROGUE PLATOON THAT WENT TOO FAR
WATCHING BABIES BEING KILLED DURING A WAR

DON'T SHUT THEM DOWN, IT CUTS LIKE A KNIFE
JUST BY LISTENING, YOU COULD SAVE A LIFE

TAKE TIME WITH THEM AND LET THEM TALK
DO SOMETHING WITH THEM, JUST GO FOR A WALK

BUT LOVE THEM, LOVE THEM, LOVE THEM PLEASE
GIVE THEM A HUG, A GENTLE SQUEEZE

BECAUSE NO ONE KNOWS HOW MANY TEARS THEY'VE CRIED
BEFORE THEY DECIDED TO COMMIT SUICIDE

THE LOSS OF A MOTHER

OUR ANGEL SPREAD HER WINGS AND GRACEFULLY SOARED ABOVE
TAKING WITH HER PRECIOUS MEMORIES AND UNCONDITIONAL LOVE

HER TIME HERE WITH US MEANT MORE THAN SHE'LL KNOW
THOUGH IT HURT US SO MUCH IT WAS TIME TO LET GO

NEVER A MEAN WORD SPOKEN SUCH A SWEET, GENTLE SOUL
WITH THE KINDEST SMILE AND A HEART OF GOLD

ALWAYS HUMBLE AND CALM NEVER RAISING HER VOICE
ALWAYS EVER SO MINDFUL WHEN MAKING A CHOICE

SHE WENT WITHOUT SO THAT OTHERS COULD HAVE
AND OFTEN GAVE WHEN SHE HAD SO LITTLE TO SPARE

SHE NURTURED, PROTECTED AND GUIDED US THROUGH LIFE
AND STOOD BY US ALL THROUGH OUR STRUGGLES AND STRIFE

NOW SHE'S EARNED HER PLACE IN HER HEAVENLY REWARD
WE MUST REJOICE IN HER PEACE FROM THIS DAY FORWARD

AND AS TIME PASSES BY AND WE THINK OF THIS DAY
WE'LL LOOK TO THE HEAVENS AND WHISPER AS WE SAY

"I LOVE YOU, I LOVE YOU AND I'LL NEVER LET GO
YOU'LL STAY IN MY HEART FOREVER MORE"

A LOT MORE LOVE

ALL OF US COME FROM GOD ABOVE
BUT MANY OF US NEED A LOT MORE LOVE

NONE OF US ARE BETTER THAN THE OTHER
IN GOD'S EYES, I'M YOUR SISTER, YOU'RE MY BROTHER

SURE, THERE ARE OTHERS WHO DON'T ACT AS WE DO
BUT THEY ARE HUMAN, JUST AS YOU

THEY MAY ACT STRANGE, OR THEY MAY SEEM ODD
BUT STILL, THEY ARE ALL CHILDREN OF GOD

TREAT THEM WITH KINDNESS AND GIVE THEM RESPECT
THEY'VE HAD ENOUGH HARDSHIPS, PAIN AND NEGLECT

THEIR ANTICS AND BEHAVIORS MAY INFURIATE YOU
BUT SO-CALLED NORMAL FOLKS DO THE SAME THING, TOO

IT'S NO LONGER HIDDEN, ITS NO LONGER TABOO
IT AFFECTS EVERYDAY PEOPLE LIKE ME AND YOU

YOU CAN'T JUST RESTRAIN THEM AGAINST THEIR WILL
OR FILL THEIR BODIES WITH NARCOTICS AND PILLS

YOU DON'T NEED A DEGREE OR SOME SPECIAL SKILL
JUST COMPASSION AND LOVE FOR THE MENTALLY ILL

I'M BEGGING AND PLEADING TO GOD ABOVE
TO PLEASE HELP US TO SHOW THEM A LOT MORE LOVE

(DEDICATED TO IRVO OTIENO AND ALL WHO SUFFER FROM MENTAL ILLNESS)

CHERISH THE MOMENTS

IT CAN COME LIKE A THIEF IN THE DARK
TEARING FRIENDS AND FAMLIES APART

ONLY YESTERDAY, YOU NEVER EVER GAVE IT A THOUGHT
NEVER THOUGHT OF THE DEVESTATION IT NOW HAS BROUGHT

IT'S PAINFUL, IT'S HEARTBREAKING WHEN IT HAPPENS SO FAST
YOU TRY TO THINK BACK, REMEMBER THE PAST

YOU REACH FOR TOMORROW, YEARN FOR YESTERDAY
THINK OF KIND WORDS THAT YOU'D LIKE TO SAY

BUT TRY AS YOU MAY, YOU CANNOT GO BACK
YOU CAN'T ACCEPT IT, BUT YES, IT'S A FACT

AS IT SINKS IN AND YOU WIPE TEARS FROM YOUR EYES
YOU ASK HOW COULD IT HAPPEN WITHOUT A GOODBYE

YESTERDAY IS OVER, IT'S ACTUALLY GONE
AS MUCH AS YOU WANT TO, YOU CAN'T HOLD ON

LET US CHERISH THE MOMENTS, ENJOY EVERY WORD SAID
BECAUSE TODAY, TONIGHT, TOMORROW THEY MAY BE DEAD

THOUGHT FOR THE DAY

WALKING THROUGH A FOREST WITHOUT SEEING THE TREES IS LIKE WANDERING THROUGH LIFE WITHOUT REALIZING YOUR BLESSINGS.

LET IT RAIN

HUSH RAINDROP DO NOT DESPAIR OF THE SORROWFUL WAILS THAT BLOW SOFTLY IN THE DISTANCE. BE THEY THE MOANING WINDS ABOVE THE DRIVING TORRENTS OR THE SAD CRIES OF THOSE WHO FEAR YOU AND SAY YOU BRING GLOOM?

SO BE IT, BUT WITHOUT YOU MIGHT OUR FIELDS BE PARCHED AND OUR BEINGS UNFED? DOES IT NOT PLEASE YOU TO SEE THE TRINKLING ARTS YOU SO KINDLY SOW AND RATHER MAKE YOU GLOW IN SPLENDOR THAT YOU MAY PRODUCE?

FEAR NOT THE RAYS OF LIGHT AT THE END OF THE STORM CAUSING YOUR BEAUTY TO VANISH. FOR A DROP OF THE HAT MAY BRING THE CLOUDS RUMBLING FORTH AND YOU SHALL RETURN IN ALL YOUR GLORY.

BUT CAREFUL, RAINDROP, TORRENTS OF DESTRUCTION YOU MAY BRING LEST YOU BE WARNED OF THE MASSIVE POWER YOU POSSESS. BE YE NOT ONE OF EARTH'S MOST MINUTE PARTICLES, YET SO ABLE TO UNLEASH A HELLISH FURY BEYOND MAN'S CONTROL?

COME, LET THY STORY BE TOLD. BRING FORTH ALL YOU MAY IN YOUR KIND AND GENTLE BLISS TO FEED THE NURTURING EARTH. YES, COME AGAIN MY FRIEND BRINGING YOUR MOIST, MYSTIC MAGIC AND FEEL THE EARTH REJOICE.

AFTER THE STORMS
(A TRIBUTE TO THE PEOPLE OF PUERTO RICO AND THE VIRGIN ISLANDS)

PUERTO RICO AND THE VIRGIN ISLANDS I'VE ADMIRED YOU FROM AFAR
AND MARVELED AT JUST HOW BEAUTIFUL YOU ARE

YOUR ANNIHILATION AND DESTRUCTION ARE SUCH A SHAME
COUPLED WITH TRAUMATIC GRIEF, AGONY AND PAIN

TO BE LEFT ON YOUR OWN IN A TIME OF DIRE NEED
IS A TRAGIC, UNFORGIVABLE ACT OF MISDEED

MY HEART WEEPS, MY SOUL CRIES TEARS OF ANGER
TO KNOW THAT YOUR PEOPLE STILL LIVE IN DANGER

I GRIEVE FOR YOU AND LONG FOR YOUR REBIRTH
A MERE PITTANCE FOR RELIEF IS NOT WHAT YOU'RE WORTH

TO YOU I SAY NEVER DOUBT IF ANYONE CARES
AND KNOW THAT YOU ARE FOREVER IN MY PRAYERS

THEY SAY TIME WILL HEAL ALL SORROW AND PAIN
JUST KNOW THAT YOUR SUFFERING HAS NOT BEEN IN VAIN

FOR YOU WILL RISE FROM THE RUINS AND SHINE LIKE A STAR
TO BE ONCE AGAIN THE RESPLENDENT BEAUTIES YOU ARE

(DEDICATED IN MEMORY OF THE VICTIMS OF THE HURRICANES OF 2017)

RAIN
(THE DESTRUCTION OF MALAWI)

IT'S BEAUTIFUL, IT'S LULLING, SO TRANQUIL TO ME
AND YET I'M ASTONISHED AT HOW IT CAN BE

A THUNDEROUS FORCE THAT'S ABLE TO KILL
LEAVING BEHIND SUFFERING AND MANY PEOPLE SO ILL

ONE DROP THAT ENABLES PLANTS TO FLOURISH
WHILE SIMULTANEOUSLY CAUSING TOWNS TO PERISH

THE DISTRESS AND DESTRUCTION THAT'S CAUSED SUCH PAIN
IT'S HARD TO BELIEVE IT WAS THE EFFECT OF RAIN

THE STRENGTH OF RAIN IS SO UNIMAGINABLE
THE DEPTH OF ITS DEVASTATION IS JUST UNBELIEVBLE

WHILE I LISTEN TO THE PATTER OF RAIN AT NIGHT
I'M ASTONISHED BY ITS AFTERMATH, A DREADFUL SIGHT

GOD HAS BLESSED ME TO SEE THE BEAUTY IN RAIN
BUT TODAY I HURT BECAUSE OTHERS ARE IN PAIN

IF THERE IS ONE THING I LONG TO SEE
IT'S A BLESSING FOR THE PEOPLE OF MALAWI

(TO THE PEOPLE OF MALWAI. YOU'RE IN MY PRAYERS.)

CONCRETE INVADERS
(THE DOWNTOWN EXPRESSWAY)

THEY SAY THEY HAD TO LEAVE THEIR HOME
THE CONCRETE INVADERS WERE ON THE ROAM

DIDN'T MATTER WHAT THEY HAD TO SAY
THAT EXPRESSWAY WAS COMING ANYWAY

DIDN'T MATTER THAT THIS WAS THEIR NEIGHBORHOOD
CITY OFFICIALS WERE DETERMINED TO DO WHAT THEY COULD

TO BUILD AN EXPRESSWAY RIGHT THROUGH THEIR LIVES
JUST TO GIVE THE PRIVILEGED SHORTER DRIVES

INSTEAD OF BUILDING THAT THING IN THE PRIVILEGED NEIGHBORHOOD
THEY FORCED THEM OUT CLAIMING IT WOULD MAKE THINGS GOOD

SOME FAMILIES HAD LIVED THERE THEIR ENTIRE LIFE
IN PEACE AND HARMONY FREE FROM STRIFE

BROKEN HEARTS AND SADNESS WERE ALL THAT WAS LEFT
SOME ELDERLY FOLKS EVEN GRIEVED THEMSELVES TO DEATH

THEY CALLED IT A PLAN, THEY CALLED IT A STRATEGY
BUT TAKING THOSE HOMES WAS MORE THAN A TRAGEDY

SOME NEVER UNDERSTOOD WHY THEY TOOK OUR NEIGHBORHOOD
WHEN THERE WERE OTHER ROUTES THAT WERE JUST AS GOOD

IT'S PLAIN AND SIMPLE, IT'S EASY TO SEE
THEY TAKE FROM PEOPLE LIKE YOU AND ME

AGE

AGE IS A NUMBER THAT'S BEEN ASSIGNED
TO DETERMINE ONE'S BEHAVIOR BY CRITERIA AND DESIGN

OF COURSE, ADULTS CAN'T WALK IN A CHILD'S SHOE
SO THERE ARE SOME THINGS THEY JUST CAN'T DO

BUT AGE IS JUST A NUMBER, AS THEY ALL SAY
AND IT SHOULD NEVER STOP YOU FROM LIVING YOUR WAY

BECAUSE YOU'RE PAST FIFTY, YOU CAN'T SLOW DOWN
YOU'VE BARELY GOTTEN YOUR FEET OFF THE GROUND

THERE'S A LOT OF GOOD LIFE THAT LIES STRAIGHT AHEAD
AND ONE MUSTN'T STOP UNTIL YOU'RE DEAD

LET NO ONE TELL YOU WHAT TO DO
IT'S YOUR LIFE, SO LIVE IT DOING WHAT YOU WANT TO

THE SAYING AGE IS JUST A NUMBER IS REALLY REAL
SO DO WHAT YOU WANT TO, DO WHAT YOU FEEL

DOESN'T MATTER IF YOU'RE NINETY-TWO
NEVER STOP DOING WHAT YOU LOVE TO DO

AND REMEMBER, YOU'RE AS YOUNG AS YOU FEEL
SO GET UP FROM THERE AND KICK UP YOUR HEELS

THE FORGOTTEN
(THE VETS)

THEY FOUGHT FOR YOU, THEY FOUGHT FOR ME
NOW THEY LIVE IN MISERY

I SEE THEM OUT THERE ON THE STREET
BEGGING AND PLEADING FOR SOMETHING TO EAT

WHILE OTHERS SIMPLY STOP AND STARE
I TRY TO GIVE WHAT I CAN SPARE

THEY GAVE EVERYTHING THEY HAD TO GIVE
ONLY TO RETURN HOME WITH NO PLACE TO LIVE

TO GET A MEAL, SOME GO TO JAIL
CAUSE LIFE ON THE STREETS IS A LIVING HELL

BILLIONS ARE SPENT BY THE GOVERNMENT EACH DAY
WHILE OUR VETS CONTINUE TO WASTE AWAY

FOR ANYONE LISTENING, I'M TAKING ALL BETS
ON WHEN THIS COUNTRY WILL REPAY ITS VETS

BLACK LIVES

I SAW THE NEWS AGAIN TODAY
ANOTHER YOUNG BLACK MAN HAS PASSED AWAY

HE WAS THE VICTIM OF SENSELESS GUN VIOLENCE
MY HEART HURT AS I GRIEVED IN SILENCE

WHEN WILL THE CYCLE OF VIOLENCE END
WHEN WILL THE BROKEN HEARTS EVER MEND

I WATCHED ANOTHER MOTHER CRY
AS SHE WIPED A TEAR FROM HER EYE

WHAT WILL IT TAKE TO STOP THE MADNESS
WHAT WILL IT TAKE TO STOP THE SADNESS

IF BLACK LIVES REALLY MATTER MY BROTHER
WHEN WILL YOU STOP KILLING EACH OTHER?

THE ULTIMATE SACRIFICE

SHE PAID THE ULTIMATE SACRIFICE

SHE GAVE HER SON, TAMIR RICE

WHAT SHE MUST HAVE FELT IS UNIMAGINABLE

WHAT HAPPENED TO HIM IS JUST UNFATHOMABLE

THE ONLY MISTAKE HE MADE THAT DAY

WAS HAVING A TOY GUN WITH WHICH TO PLAY

HE NEVER THOUGHT THAT IT WOULD CAUSE HIM TO DIE

IN A MOMENT, IN A SECOND, IN THE BLINK OF AN EYE

(DEDICATED TO THE FAMILY OF TAMIR RICE)

KAEPERNICK

KEEP LOVE

AND

ETERNAL

PEACE

ETCHED IN YOUR HEART

REMEMBER TO GIVE RESPECT

NEVER YIELD TO INJUSTICE

INCORPORATE EMPATHY AND

COMPASSION TO GIVE YOU BALANCE

KNEEL IN SILENCE WHEN YOUR HEART IS HEAVY

    WITH PAIN ON HIS FACE, HE CAPTURED ME
    ON THE FOOTBALL FIELD DOWN ON ONE KNEE

    I COULD NOT MOVE, I WAS STUCK ON PAUSE
    WATCHING THIS BROTHER KNEELING FOR A CAUSE

    I'LL NEVER FORGET THE LOOK ON HIS FACE
    JUST TRYING TO MAKE A DIFFERENCE IN THE HUMAN RACE

    (DEDICATED TO COLIN R. KAEPERNICK. YOUR FIGHT FOR
    HUMANITY WILL NEVER BE FORGOTTEN.)

WHEN WILL IT END

GUESS YOU'RE WONDERING ABOUT THIS EMPTY PAGE
AND I'M WONDERING WHY THERE'S SO MUCH RAGE...

FROM IRVO OTIENO TO EMMETT TILL
NOTHING WILL EVER FILL THE VOID I FEEL

I'M GUESSING IT WILL NEVER END...
THE SENSELESS MURDERS OF OUR BLACK MEN

(PEACE AND LOVE TO THE FAMILIES OF THESE TRAGIC KILLINGS)

A BIRD

THERE ONCE WAS A BIRD NAMED RACISM

THAT WAS HAILED FOR HIS SO-CALLED HEROISM

THEN THE FINAL DAY CAME

WHEN IT HAD NO MORE FAME

SO AWAY FLEW THE BIRD

SPEWING HARSH ANGRY WORDS

IT FLEW HIGH AND LOW AND VERY FAR

UNTIL IT WAS STRUCK BY THE HOOD OF A CAR....

AND THE WORLD WAS BETTER FOR ALL

THE TENANT

WE ALL KNOW THAT TENANT WHO REFUSES TO GET OUT
NO MATTER HOW MUCH YOU SCREAM, FUSS AND SHOUT

HE'LL STAY ON THE PREMISES AND GIVE YOU NO RELIEF
NOT A MOMENT OF PEACE, IN TIMES OF SADNESS AND GRIEF

YOU CAN'T TAKE HIM TO COURT OR THREATEN HIS LIFE
HE'LL ONLY CAUSE MORE CHAOS, CONFUSION, PAIN AND STRIFE

NO MATTER HOW YOU TRY TO SUBDUE HIM, HE CAN'T BE CAUGHT
JUST KEEPS INTERRUPTING YOU DAILY WITH EACH NEGATIVE THOUGHT

IF YOU'RE NOT CAREFUL, HE'LL GET THE BEST OF YOU
HE'LL MAKE YOU DO THINGS YOU KNOW YOU SHOULDN'T DO

HE'LL EAT AT YOU CONTINUOUSLY UNTIL YOU BREAK
CAUSING YOU ANGER AND MAKING YOU HATE

IT'S HARD TO EVICT HIM BUT MANY HAVE WON
WITH LOVE AND DISCIPLINE IT CAN BE DONE

HEED MY WARNING, LET THERE BE NO DOUBT
IF YOU LET SATAN INTO YOUR HEART, IT'S HARD TO GET HIM OUT

HOLD ON TO LOVE

POSITIVITY AND LOVE IN CONJUNCTION WITH A SMILE
WILL ALWAYS MAKE LIVING YOUR LIFE WORTH WHILE

THERE WILL BE MANY WHO WILL COME TO YOU
SEEKING TO UPSET YOU WITH THINGS THEY SAY AND DO

THEIR MISDIRECTED ANGER COMES DEEP FROM WITHIN
IT DESTROYS RELATIONSHIPS WITH FAMILIES AND FRIENDS

DON'T LET THEM STRIP YOU OF YOUR DIGNITY AND PRIDE
HOLD ON TO THE LOVE THAT YOU HAVE INSIDE

DON'T DRIVE AND DRINK

IT'S TWO A.M AS YOU GET IN YOUR CAR
KNOWING YOU SHOULDN'T BECAUSE YOU'VE JUST LEFT A BAR

VOID OF EMOTIONS, YOUR BODY REELING
IMPAIRED JUDGEMENT, YOU HAVE NO FEELING

STILL, YOU INSIST THAT YOU'RE OKAY
UNAWARE YOU MAY NOT LIVE TO SEE ANOTHER DAY

NOT ONLY DO YOU CARE WHETHER YOUR LIFE IS IN DANGER
YOU'LL CAUSE OTHERS HEART ACHE, PAIN AND ANGER

JUST TO LIVE FOR ONE MOMENT OF JOY
HOW MANY LIVES MUST YOU DESTROY

YOU'LL CRY AS YOU APOLOGIZE OVER AND OVER IN VAIN
SAYING YOU NEVER, EVER MEANT TO CAUSE SO MUCH PAIN

ALTHOUGH DRIVING DRUNK IS NOTHING NEW
BY NOW, ITS EFFECT SHOULD BE CLEAR TO YOU

WITHOUT ANY HESITATION, YOU'VE HAD YOUR FUN
NOW THE CONSEQUENCES YOU'LL PAY HAVE LEFT YOU NUMB

WHAT YOU'VE DONE WAS UNSPEAKABLE, A LIFE WAS LOST
AS DIFFICULT AS IT SEEMS, YOU MUST PAY THE COST

NO MATTER THE PRICE YOU'LL HAVE TO PAY
IT WILL NEVER COMPARE TO WHAT OTHERS FEEL TODAY

IF THIS SCENARIO HAS MADE YOU THINK
JUST MAKE A PROMISE NOT TO DRIVE AND DRINK

(DEDICATED TO ALL VICTIMS OF DRUNK DRIVERS)

ONE WISH

OUR NATION HAS A VERY, VERY SERIOUS AFFLICTION
IT'S AN AWFUL CONDITION CALLED DRUG ADDICTION

IT'S BROKEN SO MANY, MANY, MANY HEARTS
AND CONTINUES TO TEAR COUNTLESS FAMILIES APART

BE IT MOTHER, FATHER, SISTER OR BROTHER
MY HEART GOES OUT TO THOSE WHO SUFFER

I MAY NEVER KNOW WHAT IT DOES TO ONE'S LIFE
BUT THROUGH EYES OF SADNESS, I'VE SEEN THE STRIFE

IF I HAD BUT ONLY ONE WISH TO GIVE
IT WOULD BE A CURE FOR ADDICTION SO THAT MANY MAY LIVE

THE MISSING

HOW CAN A PERSON JUST DISAPPEAR?
THE THOUGHT OF SUCH CAUSES FEAR

WHETHER ABDUCTED WALKING DOWN THE STREET
OR A SMALL CHILD SNATCHED WHILE IN A CAR SEAT

WITHOUT A SECOND THOUGHT, THEY WERE TAKEN AWAY
UNAWARE THAT THEY MAY NEVER SEE ANOTHER DAY

THEIR SMILE, THEIR LAUGHTER, THEIR CARING WORDS
THE SOUND OF THEIR VOICES, NO LONGER HEARD

WITH PAIN IN THEIR HEARTS, MANY WAIT IN DISBELIEF
AS TIME GOES ON, THEIR HOPE TURNS TO GRIEF

NO PHONE CALLS, NO LETTERS, NOT EVEN A TEXT
FRIENDS AND FAMILIES WONDER WHAT COULD COME NEXT

NO ONE SHOULD SUFFER THE TERRIBLE PAIN THEY MUST FEEL
IT'S HARD TO ACCEPT, BECAUSE IT SEEMS SO UNREAL

AGAIN, I FIND MYSELF PRAYING AND WISHING
FOR A SAFE RETURN FOR ALL WHO ARE MISSING

(DEDICATED TO ALL TOUCHED BY THESE TRAGIC INCIDENTS)

SUN AND MOON

TODAY THE SUN AND THE MOON SLOWLY DANCED TOGETHER
THEY SEEMED TO SHARE A LOVE THAT WOULD LAST FOREVER

AS THEY DANCED TOGETHER IN THE HEAVENLY SKIES
THEY BLANKETED THE EARTH RIGHT BEFORE MY VERY EYES

THE SUN DANCED TO THE LEFT AND THE MOON TO THE RIGHT
FILLING THE UNIVERSE WITH UTTER DELIGHT

AS THE TWO PARTED AND WENT THEIR SEPARATE WAYS
I COULD ONLY WATCH IN AWE, I WAS SO PLEASANTLY AMAZED

SOME STILL THINK IT'S STRANGE AND EVEN SAID IT WAS ODD
BUT I'VE ALWAYS KNOWN IT WAS JUST AN ACT OF GOD

I OFFERED NO WORDS, NEVER PARTED MY LIPS
I ONLY SMILED AS THEY SPOKE OF THE "ECLIPSE"

PEACE FOR ALL MANKIND

TODAY THE EARTH MOVED
THE SUN KISSED THE HORIZON

DEWDROPS SPRINKLED HONEY-LACED TEARS UPON THE GREENERY

KIND WORDS WERE WHISPERED BY THE GOD-FEARING WINDS
LOVE AND TRUST WERE NOT SPOKEN, JUST FELT

NO TRUER HEARTS HAVE EVER FELT SO VULNERABLE AS NOW
FOR THE DIVINE WORD OF PEACE HAS ARCHED THE SKY AS A RAINBOW

COME NOW, LET US ALL JOIN TOGETHER
TRANQUILITY REIGNS

LET US NOT SPEAK OF LOVE BUT SOW ITS SEEDS IN THIS NEW AWAKENING...

PEACE

THOUGHT FOR THE DAY

MIX 1 PART KINDNESS, 1 PART COMPASSION, 1 PART YOU.
INHALE DEEPLY, THEN EXHALE SLOWLY AND
WATCH THE MAGIC BEGIN!

www.ingramcontent.com/pod-product-compliance
Lightning Source LLC
Chambersburg PA
CBHW080543090426
42734CB00016B/3191